RILEY CHILD-RHYMES

JAMES WHITCOMB RILEY

WITH

HOOSIER PICTURES

BY

WILL VAWTER

NEW WEST PRESS

Copyright © 2021 by New West Press

ISBN 978-1-64965-177-8

All rights reserved. This book or any portion thereof may not be reproduced or used in any manner whatsoever without the express written permission of the publisher except for the use of brief quotations in a book review or scholarly journal.

New West Press
Henderson, NV 89052
www.nwwst com

Ordering Information:
Special discounts are available on quantity purchases by corporations, associations, educators, and others. For details, contact the publisher at the listed address below.

U.S. trade bookstores and wholesalers: Please contact New West Press:

Tel: (480) 648-1061; or email: contact@nwwst.com

*He owns the bird-songs of the hills—
The laughter of the April rills;
In Morning's dewy coronet,—
And his the Dusk's first minted stars
That twinkle through the pasture-bars
And litter all the skies at night
With glittering scarps of silver light;—
The Rainbow's bar, from rim to rim,
In beaten gold, belongs to him.*

LITTLE ORPHANT ANNIE	1
THE RAGGEDY MAN	5
CURLY LOCKS	8
THE FUNNY LITTLE FELLOW	11
THE HAPPY LITTLE CRIPPLE	15
THE RIDER OF THE KNEE	20
DOWN AROUND THE RIVER	22
AUNTY'S HOUSE	25
THE DAYS GONE BY	28
THE BUMBLEBEE	30
THE BOY LIVES ON OUR FARM	32
THE SQUIRTGUN UNCLE MAKED ME.	35
THE OLD TRAMP.	38
OLD AUNT MARY'S	39
WINTER FANCIES	42
THE RUNAWAY BOY	45
THE LITTLE COAT	48
AN IMPETUOUS RESOLVE	51
WHO SANTY-CLAUS WUZ	52

CONTENTS

THE NINE LITTLE GOBLINS	55
TIME OF CLEARER TWITTERINGS	58
THE CIRCUS-DAY PARADE	62
THE LUGUBRIOUS WHING-WHANG	65
WAITIN' FER THE CAT TO DIE	67
NAUGHTY CLAUDE	70
THE SOUTH WIND AND THE SUN	71
THE JOLLY MILLER	79
OUR HIRED GIRL	82
THE BOYS' CANDIDATE	85
THE PET COON	86
THE OLD HAY-MOW	89
ON THE SUNNY SIDE	92
A SUDDEN SHOWER	95
GRANDFATHER SQUEERS	98
THE PIXY PEOPLE	103
A LIFE-LESSON	107
A HOME-MADE FAIRY-TALE	110
THE BEAR STORY	113
ENVOY	120

LITTLE ORPHANT ANNIE

LITTLE Orphant Annie's come to our house to stay,
An' wash the cups an' saucers up, an' brush the
   crumbs way,
An' shoo the chickens off the porch, an' dust the hearth,
      an' sweep,
An' make the fire, an' bake the bread, an' earn her board-
      an'-keep;
An' all us other childern, when the supper things is done,
We set around the kitchen fire an' has the mostest fun
A-list'nin' to the witch-tales 'at Annie tells about,
An' the Gobble-uns 'at gits you
         Ef you
            Don't
               Watch
                  Out!

Onc't they was a little boy wouldn't say his prayers,—
So when he went to bed at night, away up stairs,
His Mammy heerd him holler, an' his Daddy heerd him bawl,
An' when they turn't the kivvers down, he wasn't there at all!
An' they seeked him in the rafter-room, an' cubby-hole, an' press,
An' seeked him up the chimbly-flue, an' ever'wheres, I guess;
But all they ever found was thist his pants an' roundabout:—
An' the Gobble-uns'll git you
    Ef you
        Don't
            Watch
                Out!

An' one time a little girl 'ud allus laugh an' grin,
An' make fun of ever'one, an' all her blood an' kin;
An' onc't, when they was "company," an' ole folks was there,
She mocked 'em an' shocked 'em, an' said she didn't care!
An' thist as she kicked her heels, an' turn't to run an' hide,
They was two great big Black Things a-standin' by her side,
An' they snatched her through the ceilin' 'fore she knowed what he's about!
An' the Gobble-uns'll git you
    Ef you
        Don't
            Watch
                Out!

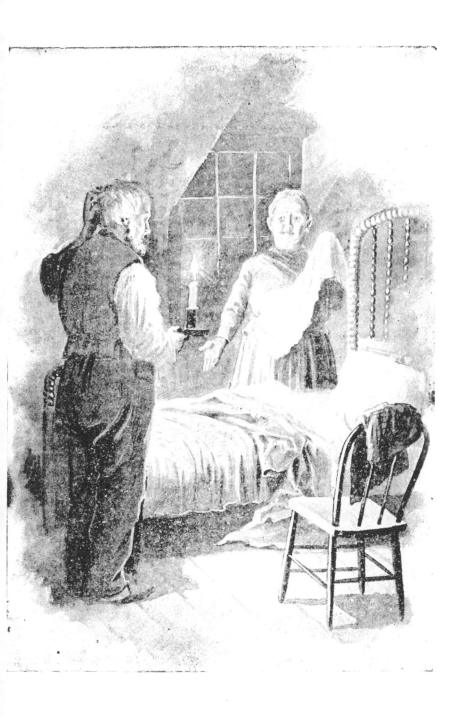

An' little Orphant Annie says when the blaze is blue,
An' the lamp-wick sputters, an' the wind goes woo-oo!
An' you hear the crickets quit, an' the moon is gray,
An' the lightnin'-bugs in dew is all squenched away,—
You better mind yer parents, an' yer teachers fond an' dear,
An' churish them 'at loves you, an' dry the orphant's tear,
An' he'p the pore an' needy ones 'at clusters all about,
Er the Gobble-uns'll git you
    Ef you
        Don't
            Watch
                Out!

THE RAGGEDY MAN

O THE RAGGEDY MAN! He works fer Pa;
An' he's the goodest man ever you saw!
He comes to our house every day,
An' waters the horses, an' feeds 'em hay;
An' he opens the shed—an' we all ist laugh
When he drives out our little old wobble-ly calf;
An' nen—ef our hired girl says he can—
He milks the cow fer 'Lizabuth Ann.—
    Aint he a' awful good Raggedy Man?
    Raggedy! Raggedy! Raggedy Man!

W'y, The Raggedy Man—he's ist so good
He splits the kindlin' an' chops the wood;
An' nen he spades in our garden, too,
An' does most things 'at boys can't do!—
He clumbed clean up in our big tree
An' shooked a' apple down fer me—

An' nother'n', too, fer 'Lizabuth Ann—
An' nother'n', too, fer The Raggedy Man.—
　Aint he a' awful kind Raggedy Man?
　　Raggedy! Raggedy! Raggedy Man!

An' The Raggedy Man, he knows most rhymes
An' tells 'em, ef I be good, sometimes:
Knows 'bout Giunts, an' Griffuns, an' Elves,
An' the Squidgicum-Squees 'at swallers therselves!
An', wite by the pump in our pasture-lot,
He showed me the hole 'at the Wunks is got,
'At lives 'way deep in the ground, an' can
Turn into me, er 'Lizabuth Ann!
　Aint he a funny old Raggedy Man?
　　Raggedy! Raggedy! Raggedy Man!

The Raggedy Man—one time when he
Wuz makin' a little bow-'n'-orry fer me,
Says "When you're big like your Pa is,
Air you go' to keep a fine store like his—
An' be a rich merchunt—an' wear fine clothes?—
Er what air you go' to be, goodness knows!"
An' nen he laughed at 'Lizabuth Ann,
An' I says "'M go' to be a Raggedy Man!—
　I'm ist go' to be a nice Raggedy Man!"
　　Raggedy! Raggedy! Raggedy Man!

CURLY LOCKS

CURLY Locks! Curly Locks! wilt thou be mine?
Thou shalt not wash the dishes, nor yet feed the swine,
But sit on a cushion and sew a fine seam,
And feast upon strawberries, sugar and cream.

Curly Locks! Curly Locks! wilt thou be mine?
The throb of my heart is in every line,
And the pulse of a passion as airy and glad
In its musical beat as the little Prince had!

Thou shalt not wash the dishes, nor yet feed the swine!—
O I'll dapple thy hands with these kisses of mine
Till the pink of the nail of each finger shall be
As a little pet blush in full blossom for me.

But sit on a cushion and sew a fine seam,
And thou shalt have fabric as fair as a dream,—
The red of my veins, and the white of my love,
And the gold of my joy for the braiding thereof.

And feast upon strawberries, sugar and cream
From a service of silver, with jewels agleam,—
At thy feet will I bide, at thy beck will I rise,
And twinkle my soul in the night of thine eyes!

Curly Locks! Curly Locks! wilt thou be mine?
Thou shalt not wash the dishes, nor yet feed the swine.—
But sit on a cushion and sew a fine seam,
And feast upon strawberries, sugar and cream.

The Funny Little Fellow.

'TWAS a Funny Little Fellow
    Of the very purest type,
For he had a heart as mellow
    As an apple over-ripe;
And the brightest little twinkle
    When a funny thing occurred,
And the lightest little tinkle
    Of a laugh you ever heard!

His smile was like the glitter
    Of the sun in tropic lands,
And his talk a sweeter twitter
    Than the swallow understands;
Hear him sing—and tell a story—
    Snap a joke—ignite a pun,—
'Twas a capture—rapture—glory,
    And explosion—all in one!

Though he hadn't any money—
    That condiment which tends
To make a fellow "honey"
    For the palate of his friends;—

Sweet simples he compounded—
    Sovereign antidotes for sin
Or taint,—a faith unbounded
    That his friends were genuine.

He wasn't honored, may be—
    For his songs of praise were slim,—
Yet I never knew a baby
    That wouldn't crow for him;
I never knew a mother
    But urged a kindly claim
Upon him as a brother,
    At the mention of his name.

The sick have ceased their sighing
    And have even found the grace
Of a smile when they were dying
    As they looked upon his face;
And I've seen his eyes of laughter
    Melt in tears that only ran
As though, swift dancing after,
    Came the Funny Little Man.

He laughed away the sorrow,
    And he laughed away the gloom
We are all so prone to borrow
    From the darkness of the tomb;
And he laughed across the ocean
    Of a happy life, and passed,

With a laugh of glad emotion,
    Into Paradise at last.

And I think the Angels knew him,
    And had gathered to await
His coming, and run to him
    Through the widely-opened Gate—
With their faces gleaming sunny
    For his laughter-loving sake,
And thinking, "What a funny
    Little Angel he will make!"

The Happy Little Cripple

I'M thist a little cripple boy, an' never goin' to grow
An' get a great big man at all!—'cause Aunty told me so.
When I was thist a baby onc't, I falled out of the bed
An' got "The Curv'ture of the Spine"—'at's what the
      Doctor said.
I never had no Mother nen—fer my Pa runned away
An' dassn't come back here no more—'cause he was drunk
      one day
An' stobbed a man in thish-ere town, an' couldn't pay his
      fine!
An' nen my Ma she died—an' I got "Curv'ture of the
      'Spine!"

I'm nine years old! An' you can't guess how much I weigh, I
      bet!—
Last birthday I weighed thirty-three!—An' I weigh thirty
      yet!
I'm awful little fer my size—I'm purt' nigh littler 'nan
Some babies is!—an' neighbors all calls me "The Little
      Man!"

15

An' Doc one time he laughed an' said: "I 'spect, first thing you know,
You'll have a little spike-tail coat an' travel with a show!"
An' nen I laughed—till I looked round an' Aunty was a-cryin'—
Sometimes she acts like that, 'cause I got "Curv'ture of the Spine."

I set—while Aunty's washin'—on my little long-leg stool,
An' watch the little boys an' girls a-skippin' by to school;
An' I peck on the winder, an' holler out an' say:
"Who wants to fight The Little Man 'at dares you all today?"
An', nen the boys climbs on the fence, an' little girls peeks through,
An' they all says: "Cause you're so big, you think we're 'feared o' you!"
An' nen they yell, an' shake their fist at me, like I shake mine—
They're thist in fun, you know, 'cause I got "Curv'ture of the Spine!"

At evening, when the ironin's done, an' Aunty's fixed the fire,
An' filled an' lit the lamp, an' trimmed the wick an' turned it higher,
An' fetched the wood all in fer night, an' locked the kitchen door,
An' stuffed the ole crack where the wind blows in up through the floor—

She sets the kittle on the coals, an' biles an' makes the tea,
An' fries the liver an' the mush, an' cooks a egg fer me;
An' sometimes—when I cough so hard—her elderberry wine
Don't go so bad fer little boys with "Curv'ture of the Spine!"

But Aunty's all so childish-like on my account, you see,
I'm 'most afeard she'll be took down—an' 'at's what bothers me!—
'Cause ef my good old Aunty ever would git sick an' die,
I don't know what she'd do in heaven—till I come, by an' by:—
Fer she's so ust to all my ways, an' ever'thing, you know,
An' no one there like me, to nuss an' worry over so!—
'Cause all the little childerns there's so straight an' strong an' fine,
They's nary angel 'bout the place with "Curv'ture of the Spine!"

THE RIDER OF THE KNEE

KNIGHTLY Rider of the Knee
Of Proud-prancing Unclery!
Gaily mount, and wave the sign
Of that mastery of thine.

Pat thy steed and turn him free,
Knightly Rider of the Knee!
Sit thy charger as a throne—
Lash him with thy laugh alone:

Sting him only with the spur
Of such wit as may occur,
Knightly Rider of the Knee,
In thy shriek of ecstasy.

Would, as now, we might endure,
Twain as one—thou miniature
Ruler, at the rein of me—
Knightly Rider of the Knee!

Down Around the River

NOON-TIME an' June-time, down around the river!
Have to furse with 'Lizey Ann— but lawzy! I fergive her!
Drives me off the place, an' says 'at all 'at she's a-wishin',
Land o' gracious! time'll come I'll git enough o' fishin'!
Little Dave, a-choppin' wood, never 'pears to notice;
Don't know where she's hid his hat, er keerin' where his
    coat is,—
Specalatin', more'n like, he haint a-goin' to mind me,
An' guessin' where, say twelve o'clock, a feller'd likely
    find me!

Noon-time an' June-time, down around the river!
Clean out o' sight o' home, an' skulkin' under kivver
Of the sycamores, jack-oaks, an' swamp-ash an' ellum—
Idies all so jumbled up, you kin hardly tell 'em!—
Tired, you know, but lovin' it, an' smilin' jes' to think 'at
Any sweeter tiredness you'd fairly want to drink it!
Tired o' fishin'—tired o' fun—line out slack an' slacker—
All you want in all the world's a little more tobacker!

Hungry, but a-hidin' it, er jes' a-not a-keerin':—
Kingfisher gittin' up an' skootin' out o' hearin';
Snipes on the t'other side, where the County Ditch is,
Wadin' up an' down the aidge like they'd rolled their britches!
Old turkle on the root kindo-sorto drappin'
Intoo th' worter like he don't know how it happen!
Worter, shade an' all so mixed, don't know which you'd orter
Say; th' worter in the shadder—shadder in the worter!

Somebody hollerin'—'way around the bend in
Upper Fork—where yer eye kin jes' ketch the endin'
Of the shiney wedge o' wake some muss-rat's a-makin'
With that pesky nose o' his! Then a sniff o' bacon,
Corn-bred an' 'dock-greens—an' little Dave a-shinnin'
'Crost the rocks an' mussel-shells, a-limpin' an' a-grinnin',
With yer dinner fer ye, an' a blessin' from the giver,
Noon-time an' June-time down around the river!

At Aunty's House

ONE time, when we'z at Aunty's house—
　'Way in the country!—where
They's ist but woods—an' pigs, an' cows—
　An' all's out-doors an' air!—
An' orchurd-swing; an' churry-trees—
An' *churries* in 'em!—Yes, an' these—
Here red-head birds steals all they please,
　An' tetch 'em ef you dare!—
W'y, wunst, one time, when we wuz there,
　We et out on the porch!

Wite where the cellar-door wuz shut
　The table wuz; an' I
Let Aunty set by me an' cut
　My vittuls up—an' pie.
'Tuz awful funny!—I could see

The red-heads in the churry-tree;
An' bee-hives, where you got to be
    So keerful, goin' by;—
An' "Comp'ny" there an' all!—an' we—
    We et out on the porch!

An' I ist et p'surves an' things
    'At Ma don't 'low me to—
An' *chickun-gizzurds*—(don't like wings
    Like *Parunts* does! do you?)
An' all the time, the wind blowed there,
An' I could feel it in my hair,
An' ist smell clover ever'where!—
    An' a' old red-head flew
Purt' nigh wite over my high-chair,
    When we et on the porch!

THE DAYS GONE BY

O THE days gone by! O the days gone by!
The apples in the orchard, and the pathway through the rye;
The chirrup of the robin, and the whistle of the quail
As he piped across the meadows sweet as any nightingale;
When the bloom was on the clover, and the blue was in the sky,
And my happy heart brimmed over, in the days gone by.

In the days gone by, when my naked feet were tripped
By the honeysuckle tangles where the water-lilies dipped,
And the ripples of the river lipped the moss along the brink,
Where the placid-eyed and lazy-footed cattle came to drink,
And the tilting snipe stood fearless of the truant's wayward cry
And the splashing of the swimmer, in the days gone by.

O the days gone by! O the days gone by!
The music of the laughing lip, the lustre of the eye;
The childish faith in fairies, and Aladdin's magic ring—
The simple, soul-reposing, glad belief in everything,—
When life was like a story, holding neither sob nor sigh,
In the golden olden glory of the days gone by.

THE BUMBLEBEE

YOU better not fool with a Bumblebee!—
    Ef you don't think they can sting—you'll see!
They're lazy to look at, an' kindo' go
Buzzin' an' bummin' aroun' so slow,
An' ac' so slouchy an' all fagged out,
Danglin' their legs as they drone about
The hollyhawks 'at they can't climb in
'Ithout ist a-tumble-un out agin!
Wunst I watched one climb clean 'way
In a jim'son-blossom, I did, one day,—
An' I ist grabbed it—an' nen let go—
An' "Ooh-ooh! Honey! I told ye so!"
Says The Raggedy Man; an' he ist run
An' pullt out the stinger, an' don't laugh none,
An' says: "They has ben folks, I guess,
'At thought I wuz predjudust, more er less,—
Yit I still muntain 'at a Bumblebee
Wears out his welcome too quick fer me!"

The Boy lives on our Farm.

THE BOY lives on our Farm, he's not
    Afeard o' horses none!
An' he can make 'em lope, er trot,
    Er rack, er pace, er run.
Sometimes he drives two horses, when
    He comes to town an' brings
A wagon-full o' 'taters nen,
    An' roastin'-ears an' things.

Two horses is "a team," he says,
    An' when you drive er hitch,
The right-un's a "near-horse," I guess
    Er "off"—I don't know which—
The Boy lives on our Farm, he told

Me, too, 'at he can see,
By lookin' at their teeth, how old
    A horse is, to a T!

I'd be the gladdest boy alive
    Ef I knowed much as that,
An' could stand up like him an' drive,
    An' ist push back my hat,
Like he comes skallyhootin' through
    Our alley, with one arm
A-wavin' Fare-ye-well! to you—
    The Boy lives on our Farm!

The Squirtgun Uncle Maked Me.

UNCLE Sidney, when he wuz here,
    Maked me a squirtgun out o' some
Elder-bushes 'at growed out near
Where wuz the brickyard—'way out clear
    To where the toll-gate come!

So when we walked back home again,
    He maked it, out in our woodhouse where
Wuz the old workbench, an' the old jack-plane,
An' the old 'pokeshave, an' the tools all lay'n'
    Ist like he wants 'em there.

He sawed it first with the old hand-saw;
    An' nen he peeled off the bark, an' got
Some glass an' scraped it; an' told 'bout Pa,
When he wuz a boy an' fooled his Ma,
    An' the whippin' 'at he caught.

Nen Uncle Sidney, he took an' filed
      A' old arn ramrod; an' one o' the ends
He screwed fast into the vise; an' smiled,
Thinkin', he said, o' when he wuz a child,
      'Fore him an' Pa wuz mens.
He punched out the peth, an' nen he put
      A plug in the end with a hole notched through;
Nen took the old drawey-knife an' cut
An' maked a handle 'at shoved clean shut
      But ist where yer hand held to.

An' he wropt th'uther end with some string an' white
      Piece o' the sleeve of a' old tored shirt;
An' nen he showed me to hold it tight,
An' suck in the water an' work it right
      An' it 'ud ist squirt an' squirt!

The Old Tramp.

A OLD Tramp slep' in our stable wuns,
   An' The Raggedy Man he caught
   An' roust him up, an' chased him off
   Clean out through our back lot!
An' th' Old Tramp hollered back an' said,—
"You're a purty man!—You air!—
With a pair o' eyes like two fried eggs,
  An' a nose like a Bartlutt pear!"

OLD AUNT MARY'S

WASN'T it pleasant, O brother mine,
In those old days of the lost sunshine
Of youth—when the Saturday's chores were through,
And the "Sunday's wood" in the kitchen, too,
And we went visiting, "me and you,"
      Out to Old Aunt Mary's?

It all comes back so clear to-day!
Though I am as bald as you are gray—
Out by the barn-lot, and down the lane,
We patter along in the dust again,
As light as the tips of the drops of the rain,
      Out to Old Aunt Mary's!

We cross the pasture, and through the wood
Where the old gray snag of the poplar stood,
Where the hammering "red-heads" hopped awry,
And the buzzard "raised" in the "clearing" sky
And lolled and circled, as we went by
      Out to Old Aunt Mary's.

And then in the dust of the road again;
And the teams we met, and the countrymen;
And the long highway, with sunshine spread
As thick as butter on country bread,
Our cares behind, and our hearts ahead
      Out to Old Aunt Mary's.

Why, I see her now in the open door,
Where the little gourds grew up the sides and o'er
The clapboard roof!—And her face—ah, me!
Wasn't it good for a boy to see—
And wasn't it good for a boy to be
        Out to Old Aunt Mary's?

And O my brother, so far away,
This is to tell you she waits to-day
To welcome us:—Aunt Mary fell
Asleep this morning, whispering, "Tell
The boys to come!" And all is well
        Out to Old Aunt Mary's.

Winter Fancies

I

WINTER without
    And warmth within;
The winds may shout
    And the storm begin;
The snows may pack
    At the window pane,
And the skies grow black,
    And the sun remain
Hidden away
    The livelong day—
But here—in here is the warmth of May!

II

Swoop your spitefullest
    Up the flue,
    Wild Winds—do!
What in the world do I care for you?
    O delightfullest
    Weather of all,

Howl and squall,
And shake the trees till the last leaves fall!

III

The joy one feels,
    In an easy chair,
Cocking his heels
    In the dancing air
That wreathes the rim of a roaring stove
Whose heat loves better than hearts can love,
    Will not permit
        The coldest day
           To drive away
The fire in his blood, and the bliss of it!

IV

Then blow, Winds, blow!
    And rave and shriek,
And snarl and snow
    Till your breath grows weak—
While here in my room
    I'm as snugly shut
As a glad little worm
    In the heart of a nut!

THE RUNAWAY BOY

WUNST I sassed my Pa, an' he
   Won't stand that, an' punished me,—
Nen when he was gone that day,
I slipped out an' runned away.

I tooked all my copper-cents,
An' clumbed over our back fence
In the jimpson-weeds 'at growed
Ever'where all down the road.

Nen I got out there, an' nen
I runned some—an' runned again
When I met a man 'at led
A big cow 'at shooked her head.

I went down a long, long lane
Where was little pigs a-play'n';
An' a grea'-big pig went "Booh!"
An' jumped up, an' skeered me too.

Nen I scampered past, an' they
Was somebody hollered "Hey!"
An' I ist looked ever'where,
An' they was nobody there.

I Want to, but I'm 'fraid to try
To go back.... An' by-an'-by
Somepin' hurts my throat inside—
An' I want my Ma—an' cried.

Nen a grea'-big girl come through
Where's a gate, an' telled me who
Am I? an' ef I tell where
My home's at she'll show me there.

But I couldn't ist but tell
What's my name; an' she says well,
An' she tooked me up an' says
She know where I live, she guess.

Nen she telled me hug wite close
Round her neck!—an' off she goes
Skippin' up the street! An' nen
Purty soon I'm home again.

An' my Ma, when she kissed me,
Kissed the big girl too, an' she
Kissed me—ef I p'omise shore
I won't run away no more!

THE LITTLE COAT

HERE'S his ragged "roundabout";
Turn the pockets inside out:
See; his pen-knife, lost to use,
Rusted shut with apple-juice;
Here, with marbles, top and string,
Is his deadly "devil-sling,"
With its rubber, limp at last
As the sparrows of the past!
Beeswax—buckles—leather straps—
Bullets, and a box of caps,—
Not a thing of all, I guess,
But betrays some waywardness—
E'en these tickets, blue and red,
For the Bible-verses said—
Such as this his mem'ry kept—
                "Jesus wept."

Here's a fishing hook-and-line,
Tangled up with wire and twine,
And dead angle-worms, and some
Slugs of lead and chewing-gum,
Blent with scents that can but come
From the oil of rhodium.
Here—a soiled, yet dainty note,
That some little sweetheart wrote,
Dotting,—"Vine grows round the stump,"
And—"My sweetest sugar lump!"

Wrapped in this—a padlock key
Where he's filed a touch-hole—see!
And some powder in a quill
Corked up with a liver pill;
And a spongy little chunk
                Of "punk."

Here's the little coat—but O!
Where is he we've censured so!
Don't you hear us calling, dear?
Back! come back, and never fear.—
You may wander where you will,
Over orchard, field and hill;
You may kill the birds, or do
Anything that pleases you!
Ah, this empty coat of his!
Every tatter worth a kiss;
Every stain as pure instead
As the white stars overhead:
And the pockets—homes were they
Of the little hands that play
Now no more—but, absent, thus
                Beckon us.

AN IMPETUOUS RESOLVE

WHEN little Dickie Swope's a man,
    He's go' to be a Sailor;
An' little Hamey Tincher, he's
    A-go' to be a Tailor:
Bud Mitchell, he's a-go' to be
    A stylish Carriage-Maker;
An' when I grow a grea'-big man,
    I'm go' to be a Baker!

An' Dick'll buy his sailor-suit
    O' Hame; and Hame'll take it
An' buy as fine a double-rigg
    As ever Bud can make it:
An' nen all three'll drive roun' fer me
    An' we'll drive off togevver,
A-slingin' pie-crust 'long the road
    Ferever an' ferever!

Who Santy-Claus Wuz

JES' a little bit o' feller—I remember still—
Ust to almost cry fer Christmas, like a youngster will.
Fourth o' July's nothin' to it!—New Year's ain't a smell!
Easter-Sunday—Circus-day—jes' all dead in the shell!
Lawzy, though! at night, you know, to set around an' hear
The old folks work the story off about the sledge an' deer,
An' "Santy" skootin' round the roof, all wrapt in fur an' fuzz—
Long afore
        I knowed who
               "Santy-Claus" wuz!

Ust to wait, an' set up late, a week er two ahead;
Couldn't hardly keep awake, ner wouldn't go to bed;
Kittle stewin' on the fire, an' Mother settin' here
Darnin' socks, an' rockin' in the skreeky rockin'-cheer;
Pap gap', an' wonder where it wuz the money went,
An' quar'l with his frosted heels, an' spill his liniment;

An' me a-dreamin' sleigh-bells when the clock 'ud whir an' buzz,
Long afore
   I knowed who
      "Santy-Claus" wuz!

Size the fire-place up an' figger how "Ole Santy" could
Manage to come down the chimbly, like they said he would;
Wisht 'at I could hide an' see him—wunderd what he'd say
Ef he ketched a feller layin' fer him thataway!
But I bet on him, an' liked him, same as ef he had
Turned to pat me on the back an' say, "Look here, my lad,
Here's my pack,—jes' he'p yourse'f, like all good boys does!"
Long afore
   I knowed who
      "Santy-Claus" wuz!

Wisht that yarn was true about him, as it 'peared to be—
Truth made out o' lies like that-un's good enough fer me!—
Wisht I still wuz so confidin' I could jes' go wild
Over hangin' up my stockin's, like the little child
Climbin' in my lap to-night, an' beggin' me to tell
'Bout them reindeers, and "Old Santy" that she loves so well
I'm half sorry fer this little-girl-sweetheart of his—
Long afore
   She knows who
      "Santy-Claus" is!

THE NINE LITTLE GOBLINS

THEY all climbed up on a high board-fence—
　　Nine little Goblins, with green-glass eyes—
Nine little Goblins that had no sense,
　　And couldn't tell coppers from cold mince pies;
　　　　And they all climbed up on the fence, and sat—
　　　　And I asked them what they were staring at.

And the first one said, as he scratched his head
　　With a queer little arm that reached out of his ear
And rasped its claws in his hair so red—
　　"This is what this little arm is fer!"
　　　　And he scratched and stared, and the next one said,
　　　　"How on earth do you scratch your head?"

And he laughed like the screech of a rusty hinge—
　　Laughed and laughed till his face grew black;
And when he choked, with a final twinge
　　Of his stifling laughter, he thumped his back
　　　　With a fist that grew on the end of his tail
　　　　Till the breath came back to his lips so pale.

And the third little Goblin leered round at me—
　　And there were no lids on his eyes at all—
And he clucked one eye, and he says, says he,

"What is the style of your socks this fall?"
    And he clapped his heels—and I sighed to see
    That he had hands where his feet should be.

Then a bald-faced Goblin, gray and grim,
    Bowed his head, and I saw him slip
His eyebrows off, as I looked at him,
    And paste them over his upper lip;
        And then he moaned in remorseful pain—
        "Would—Ah, would I'd me brows again!"

And then the whole of the Goblin band
    Rocked on the fence-top to and fro,
And clung, in a long row, hand in hand,
    Singing the songs that they used to know—
        Singing the songs that their grandsires sung
        In the goo-goo days of the Goblin-tongue.

And ever they kept their green-glass eyes
    Fixed on me with a stony stare—
Till my own grew glazed with a dread surmise,
    And my hat whooped up on my lifted hair,
        And I felt the heart in my breast snap to
        As you've heard the lid of a snuff-box do.

And they sang "You're asleep! There is no board-fence,
    And never a Goblin with green-glass eyes!—
'Tis only a vision the mind invents
    After a supper of cold mince-pies,—
        And you're doomed to dream this way," they said,—
        "And you sha'n't wake up till you're clean plum dead!"

TIME OF CLEARER TWITTERINGS

I

TIME of crisp and tawny leaves,
And of tarnished harvest sheaves,
And of dusty grasses—weeds—
Thistles, with their tufted seeds
Voyaging the Autumn breeze
Like as fairy argosies:
Time of quicker flash of wings,
And of clearer twitterings
In the grove, or deeper shade
Of the tangled everglade,—
Where the spotted water-snake
Coils him in the sunniest brake;
And the bittern, as in fright,
Darts, in sudden, slanting flight,
Southward, while the startled crane
Films his eyes in dreams again.

II

Down along the dwindled creek
We go loitering. We speak
Only with old questionings
Of the dear remembered things
Of the days of long ago,
When the stream seemed thus and so
In our boyish eyes:—The bank
Greener then, through rank on rank
Of the mottled sycamores,
Touching tops across the shores:
Here, the hazel thicket stood—
There, the almost pathless wood
Where the shellbark hickory tree
Rained its wealth on you and me.
Autumn! as you loved us then,
Take us to your heart again!

III

Season halest of the year!
How the zestful atmosphere
Nettles blood and brain, and smites
Into life the old delights
We have tasted in our youth,
And our graver years, forsooth!
How again the boyish heart
Leaps to see the chipmunk start
From the brush and sleek the sun
Very beauty, as he runs!

How again a subtle hint
Of crushed pennyroyal or mint,
Sends us on our knees, as when
We were truant boys of ten—
Brown marauders of the wood,
Merrier than Robin Hood!

IV

Ah! will any minstrel say,
In his sweetest roundelay,
What is sweeter, after all,
Than black haws, in early Fall—
Fruit so sweet the frost first sat,
Dainty-toothed, and nibbled at!
And will any poet sing
Of a lusher, richer thing
Than a ripe May-apple, rolled
Like a pulpy lump of gold
Under thumb and finger-tips,
And poured molten through the lips?
Go, ye bards of classic themes,
Pipe your songs by classic streams!
I would twang the redbird's wings
In the thicket while he sings!

THE CIRCUS-DAY PARADE

Oh, the Circus-Day parade! How the bugles played and played!
And how the glossy horses tossed their flossy manes, and neighed,
As the rattle and the rhyme of the tenor-drummer's time
Filled all the hungry hearts of us with melody sublime!

How the grand band-wagon shone with a splendor all its own,
And glittered with a glory that our dreams had never known!
And how the boys behind, high and low of every kind,
Marched in unconscious capture, with a rapture undefined!

How the horsemen, two and two, with their plumes of white and blue,
And crimson, gold and purple, nodding by at me and you.
Waved the banners that they bore, as the Knights in days of yore,
Till our glad eyes gleamed and glistened like the spangles that they wore!

How the graceless-graceful stride of the elephant was eyed,
And the capers of the little horse that cantered at his side!
How the shambling camels, tame to the plaudits of their fame,
With listless eyes came silent, masticating as they came.

How the cages jolted past, with each wagon battened fast,
And the mystery within it only hinted of at last
From the little grated square in the rear, and nosing there
The snout of some strange animal that sniffed the outer air!

And, last of all, The Clown, making mirth for all the town,
With his lips curved ever upward and his eyebrows ever down,
And his chief attention paid to the little mule that played
A tattoo on the dashboard with his heels, in the parade.

Oh! the Circus-Day parade! How the bugles played and played!
And how the glossy horses tossed their flossy manes and neighed.
As the rattle and the rhyme of the tenor-drummer's time
Filled all the hungry hearts of us with melody sublime!

The Lugubrious Whing-Whang

THE rhyme o' The Raggedy Man's 'at's best
    Is Tickle me, Love, in these Lonesome Ribs,—
'Cause that-un's the strangest of all o' the rest,
An' the worst to learn, an' the last one guessed,
An' the funniest one, an' the foolishest.—
    Tickle me, Love, in these Lonesome Ribs!

I don't know what in the world it means—
    Tickle me, Love, in these Lonesome Ribs!—
An' nen when I tell him I don't, he leans
Like he was a-grindin' on some machines
An' says: Ef I don't, w'y, I don't know beans!
    Tickle me, Love, in these Lonesome Ribs!—

Out on the margin of Moonshine Land,
    Tickle me, Love, in these Lonesome Ribs!
Out where the Whing-Whang loves to stand,
Writing his name with his tail in the sand,
And swiping it out with his oogerish hand;
    Tickle me, Love, in these Lonesome Ribs!

Is it the gibber of Gungs or Keeks?
    Tickle me, Love, in these Lonesome Ribs!
Or what is the sound that the Whing-Whang seeks?—
Crouching low by the winding creeks
And holding his breath for weeks and weeks!
    Tickle me, Love, in these Lonesome Ribs!

Aroint him the wraithest of wraithly things!
    Tickle me, Love, in these Lonesome Ribs!
'Tis a fair Whing-Whangess, with phosphor rings
And bridal-jewels of fangs and stings;
And she sits and as sadly and softly sings
As the mildewed whir of her own dead wings,—
    Tickle me, Dear,
        Tickle me here,
    Tickle me, Love, in these Lonesome Ribs!

Waitin' Fer The Cat To Die

LAWZY! don't I rickollect
    That-'air old swing in the lane!
Right and proper, I expect,
    Old times can't come back again;
But I want to state, ef they
    Could come back, and I could say
What my pick 'ud be, i jing!
    I'd say, Gimme the old swing
'Nunder the old locus'-trees
On the old place, ef you please!—
Danglin' there with half-shet eye,
Waitin' fer the cat to die!

I'd say, Gimme the old gang
Of barefooted, hungry, lean,
Ornry boys you want to hang
When you're growed up twic't as mean!
The old gyarden-patch, the old
Truants, and the stuff we stol'd!
The old stompin'-groun', where we
Wore the grass off, wild and free

As the swoop of the old swing,
Where we ust to climb and cling,
And twist roun', and fight, and lie—
Waitin' fer the cat to die!

'Pears like I 'most allus could
    Swing the highest of the crowd—
Jes sail up there tel I stood
    Downside-up, and screech out loud,—
Ketch my breath, and jes drap back
Fer to let the old swing slack,
Yit my tow-head dippin' still
In the green boughs, and the chill
Up my backbone taperin' down,
With my shadder on the ground'
Slow and slower trailin' by—
Waitin' fer the cat to die!

Now my daughter's little Jane's
    Got a kind o' baby-swing
On the porch, so's when it rains
    She kin play there—little thing!
And I'd limped out t'other day
With my old cheer this-a-way,
Swingin' her and rockin' too,
Thinkin' how I ust to do
At her age, when suddently,
"Hey, Gran'pap!" she says to me,
"Why you rock so slow?" ... Says I,
"Waitin' fer the cat to die!"

NAUGHTY CLAUDE

WHEN Little Claude was naughty wunst
    At dinner-time, an' said
He won't say "Thank you" to his Ma,
    She maked him go to bed
An' stay two hours an' not git up,—
    So when the clock struck Two,
Nen Claude says,— "Thank you, Mr. Clock,
    I'm much obleeged to you!"

The South Wind and the Sun.

O THE South Wind and the Sun
    How each loved the other one—
Full of fancy—full of folly—
    Full of jollity and fun!
    How they romped and ran about,
    Like two boys when school is out,
With glowing face, and lisping lip,
    Low laugh, and lifted shout!

    And the South Wind—he was dressed
    With a ribbon round his breast
That floated, flapped and fluttered
    In a riotous unrest;
    And a drapery of mist,
    From the shoulder and the wrist
Flowing backward with the motion
    Of the waving hand he kissed.

    And the Sun had on a crown
    Wrought of gilded thistledown,
And a scarf of velvet vapor,
    And a raveled-rainbow gown;

And his tinsel-tangled hair,
　　Tossed and lost upon the air,
With glossier and flossier
　　Than any anywhere.

　　And the South Wind's eyes were two
　　　　Little dancing drops of dew,
As he puffed his cheeks, and pursed his lips,
　　　　And blew and blew and blew!
　　　　And the Sun's—like diamond-stone,
　　　　　Brighter yet than ever known,
As he knit his brows and held his breath,
　　　　And shone and shone and shone!

　　　　And this pair of merry fays
　　　　　Wandered through the summer days;
Arm-in-arm they went together
　　　　Over heights of morning haze—
　　　　Over slanting slopes of lawn
　　　　　They went on and on and on,
Where the daisies looked like star-tracks
　　　　Trailing up and down the dawn.

　　　　And where'er they found the top
　　　　　Of a wheat-stalk droop and lop,
They chucked it underneath the chin
　　　　And praised the lavish crop,
　　　　Till it lifted with the pride
　　　　Of the heads it grew beside,

And then the South Wind and the Sun
    Went onward satisfied.

    Over meadow-lands they tripped,
    Where the dandelions dipped
In crimson foam of clover bloom
    And dripped and dripped and dripped!
    And they clinched the bumble-stings,
    Gauming honey on their wings,
And bundling them in lily-bells,
    With maudlin murmurings.

    And the humming-bird, that hung
    Like a jewel up among
The tilted honeysuckle horns,
    They mesmerized and swung
    In the palpitating air,
    Drowsed with odors strange and rare,
And, with whispered laughter, slipped away,
    And left him hanging there.

    And they braided blades of grass
    Where the truant had to pass;
And they wriggled through the rushes
    And the reeds of the morass,
    Where they danced, in rapture sweet,
    O'er the leaves that laid a street
Of undulant mosaic for
    The touches of their feet.

By the brook with mossy brink,
    Where the cattle came to drink,
They trilled and piped and whistled
    With the thrush and bobolink,
    Till the kine, in listless pause,
    Switched their tails in mute applause,
With lifted heads, and dreamy eyes,
    And bubble-dripping jaws.

    And where the melons grew,
    Streaked with yellow, green and blue,
These jolly sprites went wandering
    Through spangled paths of dew;
    And the melons, here and there,
    They made love to, everywhere,
Turning their pink souls to crimson
    With caresses fond and fair.

    Over orchard walls they went,
    Where the fruited boughs were bent
Till they brushed the sward beneath them
    Where the shine and shadow blent;
    And the great green pear they shook
    Till the sallow hue forsook
Its features, and the gleam of gold
    Laughed out in every look.

    And they stroked the downy cheek
    Of the peach, and smoothed it sleek,

And flushed it into splendor;
    And, with many an elfish freak,
    Gave the russet's rust a wipe—
    Prankt the rambo with a stripe,
And the winesap blushed its reddest
    As they spanked the pippins ripe.

    Through the woven ambuscade
    That the twining vines had made,
They found the grapes, in clusters,
    Drinking up the shine and shade—
    Plumpt, like tiny skins of wine,
    With a vintage so divine
That the tongue of Fancy tingled
    With the tang of muscadine.

    And the golden-banded bees,
    Droning o'er the flowery leas,
They bridled, reined, and rode away
    Across the fragrant breeze,
    Till in hollow oak and elm
    They had groomed and stabled them
In waxen stalls that oozed with dews
    Of rose and lily-stem.

    Where the dusty highway leads,
    High above the wayside weeds,
They sowed the air with butterflies
    Like blooming flower-seeds,

Till the dull grasshopper sprung
    Half a man's-height up, and hung
Tranced in the heat, with whirring wings,
    And sung and sung and sung!

And they loitered, hand in hand,
    Where the snipe along the sand
Of the river ran to meet them
    As the ripple meets the land,
    Till the dragonfly, in light
    Gauzy armor, burnished bright,
Came tilting down the waters
    In a wild, bewildered flight.

And they heard the kildee's call,
    And afar, the waterfall,
But the rustle of a falling leaf
    They heard above it all;
    And the trailing willow crept
    Deeper in the tide that swept
The leafy shallop to the shore,
    And wept and wept and wept!

And the fairy vessel veered
    From its moorings—tacked and steered
For the center of the current—
    Sailed away and disappeared:
    And the burthen that it bore
    From the long-enchanted shore—

"Alas! the South Wind and the Sun!"
    I murmur evermore.

    For the South Wind and the Sun,
    Each so loves the other one,
For all his jolly folly,
    And frivolity and fun,
    That our love for them they weigh
    As their fickle fancies may,
And when at last we love them most,
    They laugh and sail away.

IT was a Jolly Miller lived on the River Dee;
   He looked upon his piller, and there he found a flea:
     "O Mr. Flea! you have bit' me,
       And you shall shorely die!"
     So he scrunched his bones against the stones—
       And there he let him lie!

Twas then the Jolly Miller he laughed and told his wife,
And she laughed fit to kill her, and dropped her carvin'-knife!—
     "O Mr. Flea!" "Ho-ho!" "Tee-hee!"
       They both laughed fit to kill,
     Until the sound did almost drownd
       The rumble of the mill!

'Laugh on, my Jolly Miller! and Missus Miller, too!—
But there's a weeping-willer will soon wave over you!"
     The voice was all so awful small—
       So very small and slim!—

He durst' infer that it was her,
    Ner her infer 'twas him!

That night the Jolly Miller, says he, "It's Wifey dear,
That cat o' yourn, I'd kill her!—her actions is so queer,—
    She rubbin' 'ginst the grindstone-legs,
      And yowlin' at the sky—
    And I 'low the moon haint greener
      Than the yaller of her eye!"

And as the Jolly Miller went chuckle-un to bed,
Was Somepin jerked his piller from underneath his head!
    "O Wife," says he, on-easi-lee,
      "Fetch here that lantern there!"
    But Somepin moans in thunder tones,
      "You tetch it ef you dare!"

'Twas then the Jolly Miller he trimbled and he quailed—
And his wife choked until her breath come back, 'n' she wailed
    And "O!" cried she, "it is the Flea,
      All white and pale and wann—
    He's got you in his clutches, and
      He's bigger than a man!"

"Ho! ho! my Jolly Miller," (fer 'twas the Flea, fer shore!)
"I reckon you'll not rack my bones ner scrunch 'em any more!"
    And then the Ghost he grabbed him clos't,
      With many a ghastly smile,
    And from the doorstep stooped and hopped
      About four hundred mile!

OUR HIRED GIRL

OUR hired girl, she's 'Lizabuth Ann;
    An' she can cook best things to eat!
She ist puts dough in our pie-pan,
    An' pours in somepin' 'at's good and sweet,
An' nen she salts it all on top
With cinnamon; an' nen she'll stop
    An' stoop an' slide it, ist as slow,
In th' old cook-stove, so's 'twon't slop
    An' git all spilled; nen bakes it, so
    It's custard pie, first thing you know!
        An' nen she'll say:
"Clear out o' my way!
They's time fer work, an' time fer play!—
    Take yer dough, an' run, Child; run!
    Er I cain't git no cookin' done!"

When our hired girl 'tends like she's mad,
    An' says folks got to walk the chalk
When she's around, er wisht they had,
    I play out on our porch an' talk
To th' Raggedy Man 'at mows our lawn;
An' he says "Whew!" an' nen leans on
    His old crook-scythe, and blinks his eyes

An' sniffs all around an' says,— "I swawn!
   Ef my old nose don't tell me lies,
It 'pears like I smell custard-pies!"
     An' nen he'll say,—
"'Clear out' o' my way!
They's time fer work an' time fer play!
    Take yer dough, an' run, Child; run!
    Er she cain't git no cookin' done!'"

Wunst our hired girl, one time when she
   Got the supper, an' we all et,
An' it was night, an' Ma an' me
   An' Pa went wher' the "Social" met,—
An' nen when we come home, an' see
A light in the kitchen-door, an' we
   Heerd a maccordeum, Pa says "Lan'—
O'Gracious! who can her beau be?"
   An' I marched in, an' 'Lizabuth Ann
   Wuz parchin' corn fer the Raggedy Man!
    Better say
"Clear out o' the way!
They's time fer work, an' time fer play!
    Take the hint, an' run, Child; run!
    Er we cain't git no courtin' done!'"

THE BOYS' CANDIDATE.

L AS' time 'at Uncle Sidney come,
    He bringed a watermelon home—
      An' half the boys in town,
Come taggin' after him.—An' he
Says, when we et it,— "Gracious me!
    'S the boy-house fell down?"

The Pet Coon

NOEY Bixler ketched him, and fetched him in to me
    When he's ist a little teenty-weenty baby-coon
'Bout as big as little pups, an' tied him to a tree;
    An' Pa gived Noey fifty cents, when he come home at noon.
Nen he buyed a chain fer him, an' little collar, too,
    An' sawed a hole in a' old tub an' turnt it upside-down;
An' little feller'd stay in there and won't come out fer you—
    'Tendin' like he's kindo' skeered o' boys 'at lives in town.

Now he aint afeard a bit! he's ist so fat an' tame,
    We on'y chain him up at night, to save the little chicks.
Holler "Greedy! Greedy!" to him, an' he knows his name,
    An' here he'll come a-waddle-un, up fer any tricks!
He'll climb up my leg, he will, an' waller in my lap,
    An' poke his little black paws 'way in my pockets where

They's beechnuts, er chinkypins, er any little scrap
    Of anything, 'at's good to eat—an' he don't care!

An' he's as spunky as you please, an' don't like dogs at all.—
    Billy Miller's black-an'-tan tackled him one day,
An' "Greedy" he ist kindo' doubled all up like a ball,
    An' Billy's dog he gived a yelp er two an' runned away!
An' nen when Billy fighted me, an' hit me with a bone,
    An' Ma she purt'nigh ketched him as he dodged an' skooted thro'
The fence, she says, "You better let my little boy alone,
    Er 'Greedy,' next he whips yer dog, shall whip you, too!"

The Old Hay-Mow

THE Old Hay-mow's the place to play
Fer boys, when it's a rainy day!
I good-'eal ruther be up there
Than down in town, er anywhere!

When I play in our stable-loft,
The good old hay's so dry an' soft,
An' feels so fine, an' smells so sweet,
I 'most ferget to go an' eat.

An' one time wunst I did ferget
To go 'tel dinner was all et,—
An' they had short-cake—an'—Bud he
Hogged up the piece Ma saved fer me!

Nen I won't let him play no more
In our hay-mow where I keep store
An' got hen-eggs to sell,—an' shoo
The cackle-un old hen out, too!

An' nen, when Aunty she was here
A-visitun from Rensselaer,
An' bringed my little cousin,—he
Can come up there an' play with me.

But, after while—when Bud he bets
'At I can't turn no summersetts,—
I let him come up, ef he can
Ac' ha'f-way like a gentleman!

ON THE SUNNY SIDE

HI and whoop-hooray, boys!
Sing a song of cheer!
Here's a holiday, boys,
Lasting half a year!
Round the world, and half is
Shadow we have tried;
Now we're where the laugh is,—
On the sunny side!

Pigeons coo and mutter,
Strutting high aloof
Where the sunbeans flutter
Through the stable roof.
Hear the chickens cheep, boys,
And the hen with pride
Clucking them to sleep, boys,
On the sunny side!

Hear the clacking guinea;
Hear the cattle moo;
Hear the horses whinny,
Looking out at you!

On the hitching-block, boys,
Grandly satisfied,
See the old peacock, boys,
On the sunny side!

Robins in the peach-tree;
Bluebirds in the pear;
Blossoms over each tree
In the orchard there!
All the world's in joy, boys,
Glad and glorified
As a romping boy, boys,
On the sunny side!

Where's a heart as mellow?
Where's a soul as free?
Where is any fellow
We would rather be?
Just ourselves or none, boys,
World around and wide,
Laughing in the sun, boys,
On the sunny side!

A Sudden Shower

BAREFOOTED boys scud up the street
    Or skurry under sheltering sheds;
And schoolgirl faces, pale and sweet,
    Gleam from the shawls about their heads.

Doors bang; and mother-voices call
    From alien homes; and rusty gates
Are slammed; and high above it all,
    The thunder grim reverberates.

And then, abrupt,—the rain! the rain!—
    The earth lies gasping; and the eyes
Behind the streaming window-pane
    Smile at the trouble of the skies.

The highway smokes; sharp echoes ring;
    The cattle bawl and cowbells clank;
And into town comes galloping
    The farmer's horse, with streaming flank.

The swallow dips beneath the eaves,
    And flirts his plumes and folds his wings;
And under the catawba leaves
    The caterpillar curls and clings.

The bumble-bee is pelted down
    The wet stem of the hollyhock;
And sullenly, in spattered brown,
    The cricket leaps the garden walk.

Within, the baby claps his hands
    And crows with rapture strange and vague;
Without, beneath the rosebush stands
    A dripping rooster on one leg.

GRANDFATHER SQUEERS

"MY grandfather Squeers," said The Raggedy Man,
As he solemnly lighted his pipe and began—

"The most indestructible man, for his years,
And the grandest on earth, was my grandfather Squeers!

"He said, when he rounded his three-score-and-ten,
'I've the hang of it now and can do it again!'

"He had frozen his heels so repeatedly, he
Could tell by them just what the weather would be;

"And would laugh and declare, 'while the Almanac would
Most falsely prognosticate, he never could!'

"Such a hale constitution had grandfather Squeers
That, 'though he'd used 'navy' for sixty odd years,

"He still chewed a dime's-worth six days of the week,
While the seventh he passed with a chew in each cheek:

"Then my grandfather Squeers had a singular knack
Of sitting around on the small of his back,

"With his legs like a letter Y stretched o'er the grate
Wherein 'twas his custom to ex-pec-tor-ate.

"He was fond of tobacco in manifold ways,
And would sit on the door-step, of sunshiny days,

"And smoke leaf-tobacco he'd raised strictly for
The pipe he'd used all through The Mexican War."

And The Raggedy Man said, refilling the bowl
Of his own pipe and leisurely picking a coal

From the stove with his finger and thumb, "You can see
What a tee-nacious habit he's fastened on me!

"And my grandfather Squeers took a special delight
In pruning his corns every Saturday night

"With a horn-handled razor, whose edge he excused
By saying 'twas one that his grandfather used;

"And, though deeply etched in the haft of the same
Was the ever-euphonious Wostenholm's name,

"'Twas my grandfather's custom to boast of the blade
As 'A Seth Thomas razor—the best ever made!'

"No Old Settlers' Meeting, or Pioneers' Fair,
Was complete without grandfather Squeers in the chair

"To lead off the programme by telling folks how
'He used to shoot deer where the Court-House stands now'—

"How 'he felt, of a truth, to live over the past,
When the country was wild and unbroken and vast,

"'That the little log cabin was just plenty fine
For himself, his companion, and fambly of nine!—

"'When they didn't have even a pump, or a tin,
But drunk surface-water, year out and year in,

"'From the old-fashioned gourd that was sweeter, by odds,
Than the goblets of gold at the lips of the gods!'"

Then The Raggedy Man paused to plaintively say
It was clockin' along to'rds the close of the day—

And he'd ought to get back to his work on the lawn,—
Then dreamily blubbered his pipe and went on:

"His teeth were imperfect—my grandfather owned
That he couldn't eat oysters unless they were 'boned';

"And his eyes were so weak, and so feeble of sight,
He couldn't sleep with them unless, every night,

"He put on his spectacles—all he possessed,—
Three pairs—with his goggles on top of the rest.

"And my grandfather always, retiring at night,
Blew down the lamp-chimney to put out the light;

"Then he'd curl up on edge like a shaving, in bed,
And puff and smoke pipes in his sleep, it is said:

"And would snore oftentimes as the legends relate,
Till his folks were wrought up to a terrible state,—

"Then he'd snort, and rear up, and roll over; and there,
In the subsequent hush they could hear him chew air.

"And so glaringly bald was the top of his head
That many's the time he has musingly said,

"As his eyes journeyed o'er its reflex in the glass,—
'I must set out a few signs of Keep Off the Grass!'

"So remarkably deaf was my grandfather Squeers
That he had to wear lightning-rods over his ears

"To even hear thunder—and oftentimes then
He was forced to request it to thunder again."

The Pixy People.

It was just a very
    Merry fairy dream!—
All the woods were airy
    With the gloom and gleam;
Crickets in the clover
    Clattered clear and strong,
And the bees droned over
    Their old honey-song.

In the mossy passes,
    Saucy grasshoppers
Leapt about the grasses
    And the thistle-burs;
And the whispered chuckle
    Of the katydid
Shook the honeysuckle
    Blossoms where he hid.

Through the breezy mazes
    Of the lazy June,
Drowsy with the hazes

Of the dreamy noon,
Little Pixy people
　　Winged above the walk,
Pouring from the steeple
　　Of a mullein-stalk.

One—a gallant fellow—
　　Evidently King,—
Wore a plume of yellow
　　In a jewelled ring
On a pansy bonnet,
　　Gold and white and blue,
With the dew still on it,
　　And the fragrance, too.

One—a dainty lady,—
　　Evidently Queen,—
Wore a gown of shady
　　Moonshine and green,
With a lace of gleaming
　　Starlight that sent
All the dewdrops dreaming
　　Everywhere she went.

One wore a waistcoat
　　Of roseleaves, out and in,
And one wore a faced-coat
　　Of tiger-lily-skin;
And one wore a neat coat

    Of palest galingale;
And one a tiny street-coat,
    And one a swallow-tail.

And Ho! sang the King of them,
    And Hey! sang the Queen;
And round and round the ring of them
    Went dancing o'er the green;
And Hey! sang the Queen of them,
    And Ho! sang the King—
And all that I had seen of them
    —Wasn't anything!

It was just a very
    Merry fairy dream!—
All the woods were airy
    With the gloom and gleam;
Crickets in the clover
    Clattered clear and strong,
And the bees droned over
    Their old honey-song!

A LIFE-LESSON

THERE! little girl; don't cry!
    They have broken your doll, I know;
       And your tea-set blue,
       And your play-house, too,
    Are things of the long ago;
       But childish troubles will soon pass by.—
          There! little girl; don't cry!

There! little girl; don't cry!
    They have broken your slate, I know;
        And the glad, wild ways
        Of your school-girl days
    Are things of the long ago;
        But life and love will soon come by.—
        There! little girl; don't cry!

There! little girl; don't cry!
    They have broken your heart, I know;
        And the rainbow gleams
        Of your youthful dreams
    Are things of the long ago;
        But Heaven holds all for which you sigh.—
        There! little girl; don't cry!

A Home-Made Fairy-Tale

BUD, come here to your Uncle a spell,
And I'll tell you something you mustn't tell—
For it's a secret and shore-nuff true,
And maybe I oughtn't to tell it to you!—
But out in the garden, under the shade
Of the apple-trees where we romped and played
Till the moon was up, and you thought I'd gone
Fast asleep.—That was all put on!
For I was a-watchin' something queer
Goin' on there in the grass, my dear!
'Way down deep in it, there I see
A little dude-Fairy who winked at me,
And snapped his fingers, and laughed as low
And fine as the whine of a mus-kee-to!
I kept still—watchin' him closer—and
I noticed a little guitar in his hand,
Which he leant 'ginst a little dead bee—and laid
His cigarette down on a clean grass-blade;
And then climbed up on the shell of a snail—

Carefully dusting his swallowtail—
And pulling up, by a waxed web-thread,
This little guitar, you remember, I said!
And there he trinkled and trilled a tune—
"My Love, so Fair, Tans in the Moon!"
Till presently, out of the clover-top
He seemed to be singing to, came k'pop!
The purtiest, daintiest Fairy face
In all this world, or any place!
Then the little ser'nader waved his hand,
As much as to say, "We'll excuse you!" and
I heard, as I squinted my eyelids to,
A kiss like the drip of a drop of dew!

THE BEAR STORY

THAT ALEX "IST MAKED UP HIS-OWN-SE'F"

W'Y, wunst they wuz a Little Boy went out
   In the woods to shoot a Bear. So, he went out
'Way in the grea'-big woods—he did.—An' he
Wuz goin' along—an' goin' along, you know,
An' purty soon he heerd somepin' go "Wooh!"—
Ist thataway— "Woo-ooh!" An' he wuz skeered,
He wuz. An' so he runned an' clumbed a tree—
A grea'-big tree, he did,—a sicka-more tree.
An' nen he heerd it ag'in: an' he looked round,
An' 't'uz a Bear!—a grea'-big shore-nuff Bear!—
No: 't'uz two Bears, it wuz—two grea'-big Bears—
One of 'em wuz—ist one's a grea'-big Bear.—
But they ist boff went "Wooh!"—An' here they come
To climb the tree an' git the Little Boy
An' eat him up!

An' nen the Little Boy
He 'uz skeered worse'n ever! An' here come
The grea'-big Bear a-climbin' th' tree to git
The Little Boy an' eat him up—Oh, no!—
It 'uzn't the Big Bear 'at clumb the tree—
It 'uz the Little Bear. So here he come
Climbin' the tree—an' climbin' the tree! Nen when
He git wite clos't to the Little Boy, w'y nen
The Little Boy he ist pulled up his gun
An' shot the Bear, he did, an' killed him dead!
An' nen the Bear he falled clean on down out
The tree—away clean to the ground, he did—
Spling-splung! he falled plum down, an' killed him, too!
An' lit wite side o' where the Big Bear's at.

An' nen the Big Bear's awful mad, you bet!—
'Cause—'cause the Little Boy he shot his gun
An' killed the Little Bear.—'Cause the Big Bear
He—he 'uz the Little Bear's Papa.—An' so here
He come to climb the big old tree an' git
The Little Boy an' eat him up! An' when
The Little Boy he saw the grea'-big Bear
A-comin', he uz badder skeered, he wuz,
Than any time! An' so he think he'll climb
Up higher—'way up higher in the tree
Than the old Bear kin climb, you know.—But he—
He can't climb higher 'an old Bears kin climb,—
'Cause Bears kin climb up higher in the trees
Than any little Boys in all the Wo-r-r-ld!

An' so here come the grea'-big-Bear, he did,—
A-climbin' up—an' up the tree, to git
The Little Boy an' eat him up! An' so
The Little Boy he clumbed on higher, an' higher,
An' higher up the tree—an' higher—an' higher—
An' higher'n iss-here house is!—An' here come
Th' old Bear—clos'ter to him all the time!—
An' nen—first thing you know,—when th' old Big Bear
Wuz wite clos't to him—nen the Little Boy
Ist jabbed his gun wite in the old Bear's mouf
An' shot an' killed him dead!—No; I fergot,—
He didn't shoot the grea'-big Bear at all—
'Cause they 'uz no load in the gun, you know—
'Cause when he shot the Little Bear, w'y, nen
No load 'uz anymore nen in the gun!

But th' Little Boy clumbed higher up, he did—
He clumbed lots higher—an' on up higher—an' higher
An' higher—tel he ist can't climb no higher,
'Cause nen the limbs 'uz all so little, 'way
Up in the teeny-weeny tip-top of
The tree, they'd break down wiv him ef he don't
Be keerful! So he stop an' think: An' nen
He look around—An' here come th' old Bear!

An' so the Little Boy make up his mind
He's got to ist git out o' there some way!—
'Cause here come the old Bear!—so clos't, his bref's
Purt 'nigh so's he kin feel how hot it is

Ag'inst his bare feet—ist like old "Ring's" bref
When he's ben out a-huntin' an's all tired.
So when th' old Bear's so clos't—the Little Boy
Ist gives a grea'-big jump fer 'nother tree—
No!—no he don't do that!—I tell you what
The Little Boy does:—W'y, nen—w'y, he—Oh, yes—
The Little Boy he finds a hole up there
'At's in the tree—an' climbs in there an' hides—
An' nen th' old Bear can't find the Little Boy
At all!—But, purty soon th' old Bear finds
The Little Boy's gun 'at's up there—'cause the gun
It's too tall to tooked wiv him in the hole.
So, when the old Bear fin' the gun, he knows
The Little Boy's ist hid 'round somers there,—
An' th' old Bear 'gins to snuff an' sniff around,
An' sniff an' snuff around—so's he kin find
Out where the Little Boy's hid at.—An' nen—nen—
Oh, yes!—W'y, purty soon the old Bear climbs
'Way out on a big limb—a grea'-long limb,—
An' nen the Little Boy climbs out the hole
An' takes his ax an' chops the limb off!... Nen
The old Bear falls k-splunge! clean to the ground
An' bust an' kill hisse'f plum dead, he did!

An' nen the Little Boy he git his gun
An' 'menced a-climbin' down the tree ag'in—
No!—no, he didn't git his gun—'cause when
The Bear falled, nen the gun falled, too—An' broked
It all to pieces, too!—An' nicest gun!—

His Pa ist buyed it!—An' the Little Boy
Ist cried, he did; an' went on climbin' down
The tree—an' climbin' down—an' climbin' down!—
An'-sir! when he 'uz purt'-nigh down,—w'y, nen
The old Bear he jumped up ag'in—an' he
Ain't dead at all—ist 'tendin' thataway,
So he kin git the Little Boy an' eat
Him up! But the Little Boy he 'uz too smart
To climb clean down the tree.—An' the old Bear
He can't climb up the tree no more—'cause when
He fell, he broke one of his—he broke all
His legs!—an' nen he couldn't climb! But he
Ist won't go'way an' let the Little Boy
Come down out of the tree. An' the old Bear
Ist growls 'round there, he does—ist growls an' goes
"Wooh!—woo-ooh!" all the time! An' Little Boy
He haf to stay up in the tree—all night—
An' 'thout no supper neether!—On'y they
Wuz apples on the tree!—An' Little Boy
Et apples—ist all night—an' cried—an' cried!
Nen when 'tuz morning th' old Bear went "Wooh!"
Ag'in, an' try to climb up in the tree
An' git the Little Boy.—But he can't
Climb t'save his soul, he can't!—An' oh! he's mad!—
He ist tear up the ground! an' go "Woo-ooh!"
An'—Oh, yes!—purty soon, when morning's come
All light—so's you kin see, you know,—w'y, nen
The old Bear finds the Little Boy's gun, you know,
'At's on the ground.—(An' it ain't broke at all—

I ist said that!) An' so the old Bear think
He'll take the gun an' shoot the Little Boy:—
But Bears they don't know much 'bout shootin' guns;
So when he go to shoot the Little Boy,
The old Bear got the other end the gun
Ag'in' his shoulder, 'stid o' th' other end—
So when he try to shoot the Little Boy,
It shot the Bear, it did—an' killed him dead!
An' nen the Little Boy clumb down the tree
An' chopped his old woolly head off:—Yes, an' killed
The other Bear ag'in, he did—an' killed
All boff the bears, he did—an' tuk 'em home
An' cooked 'em, too, an' et 'em!
—An' that's all.

ENVOY

MANY pleasures of youth have been buoyantly sung—
    And, borne on the winds of delight, may they beat
With their palpitant wings at the hearts of the Young,
    And in bosoms of Age find as warm a retreat!—
Yet sweetest of all of the musical throng,
    Though least of the numbers that upward aspire,
Is the one rising now into wavering song,
    As I sit in the silence and gaze in the fire.

'Tis a Winter long dead that beleaguers my door
    And muffles his steps in the snows of the past:
And I see, in the embers I'm dreaming before,
    Lost faces of love as they looked on me last:—
The round, laughing eyes of the desk-mate of old
    Gleam out for a moment with truant desire—
Then fade and are lost in a City of Gold,
    As I sit in the silence and gaze in the fire.

And then comes the face, peering back in my own,
    Of a shy little girl, with her lids drooping low,
As she faltering tells, in a far-away tone,
    The ghost of a story of long, long ago.—
Then her dewy blue eyes they are lifted again;
    But I see their glad light slowly fail and expire,
As I reach and cry to her in vain, all in vain!—
    As I sit in the silence and gaze in the fire.

Then the face of a Mother looks back, through the mist
    Of tears that are welling; and, lucent with light,
I see the dear smile of the lips I have kissed
    As she knelt by my cradle at morning and night;
And my arms are outheld, with a yearning too wild
    For any but God in His love to inspire,
As she pleads at the foot of His throne for her child,—
    As I sit in the silence and gaze in the fire.

O pathos of rapture! O glorious pain!
    My heart is a blossom of joy over-run
With a shower of tears, as a lily with rain
    That weeps in the shadow and laughs in the sun.
The blight of the frost may descend on the tree,
    And the leaf and the flower may fall and expire,
But ever and ever love blossoms for me,
    As I sit in the silence and gaze in the fire.